Alfred's Basic Piano Library

Praise Hits • Level 1B

P i a n o

Arranged by Tom Gerou

This series answers the often expressed need for contemporary Christian music to be used as supplementary pieces for students. Soon after beginning piano study, students can play attractive versions of the best-known praise music of today.

Included with most titles in Level 1B is a teacher duet. Not only do the duets add harmony and rhythmic structure to the solos, but they also teach students the "give and take" of working together in a collaborative performance.

This book is correlated page-by-page with Lesson Book 1B of *Alfred's Basic Piano Library*; pieces should be assigned based on the instructions in the upper-right corner of each title page of *Praise Hits.* Since the melodies and rhythms of praise music do not always lend themselves to precise grading, you may find that these pieces are sometimes a little longer and more difficult than the corresponding pages in the Lesson Book. The teacher's judgment is the most important factor in deciding when to assign each arrangement.

When the books in the *Praise Hits* series are assigned in conjunction with the Lesson Books, these appealing pieces reinforce new concepts as they are introduced. In addition, the motivation the music provides could not be better. The emotional satisfaction that students receive from mastering each praise song increases their enthusiasm to begin the next one.

Alfred Music
P.O. Box 10003
Van Nuys, CA 91410-0003
alfred.com

Produced in USA.

ISBN-10: 0-7390-9238-3
ISBN-13: 978-0-7390-9238-5

Cover Photos
Meadow at morning: © Shutterstock.com / Galyna Andrushko • Deco sun: © Shutterstock.com / Mark Grenier

Use with Alfred's Basic Piano Library
Lesson Book 1B, after page 11.

Worthy, You Are Worthy

Words and Music by Don Moen
Arr. by Tom Gerou

DUET PART (Student plays 1 octave higher.)

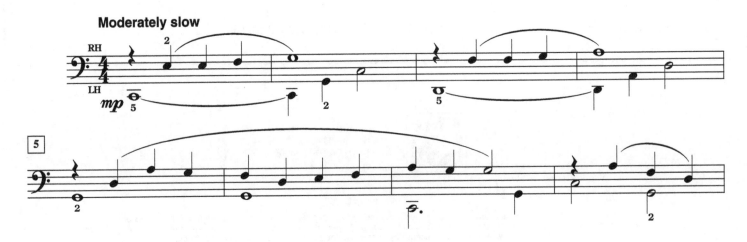

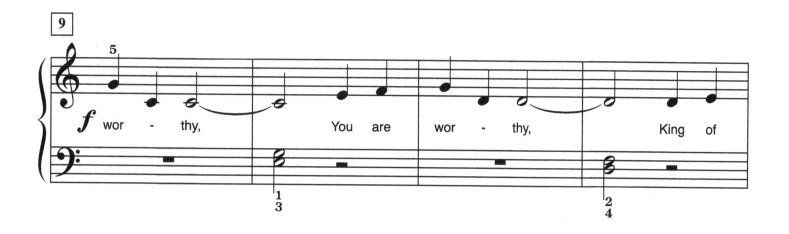

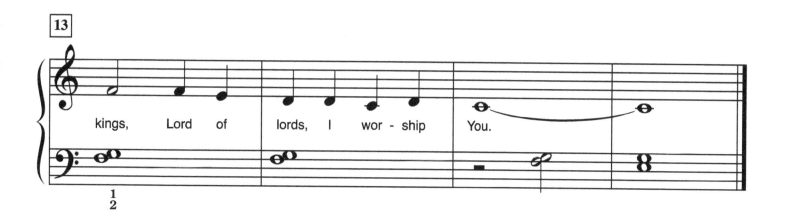

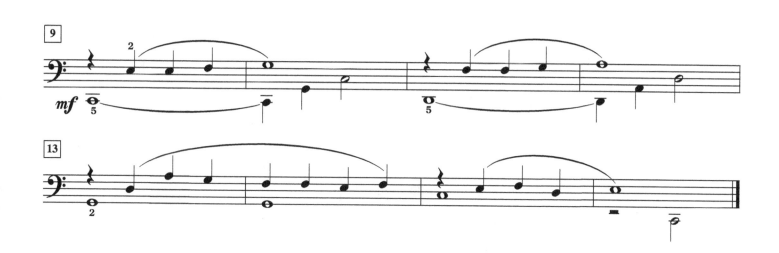

4

Blessed Be the Name of the Lord

Words and Music by Don Moen
Arr. by Tom Gerou

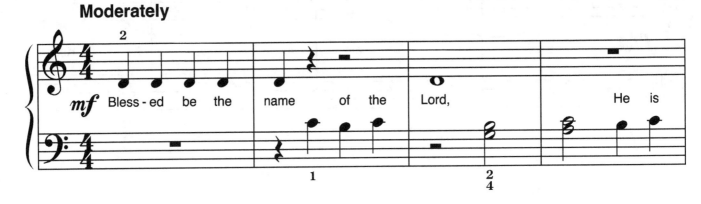

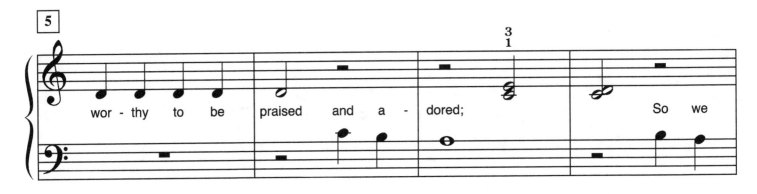

DUET PART (Student plays 1 octave higher.)

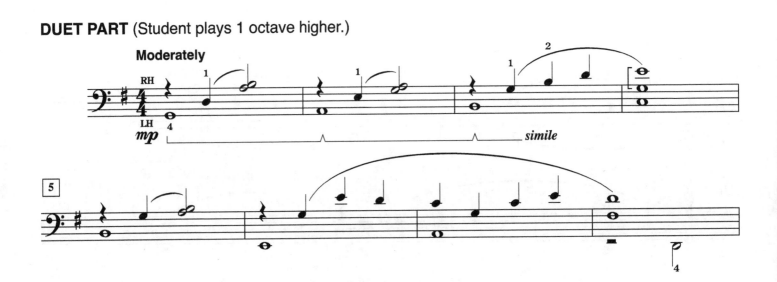

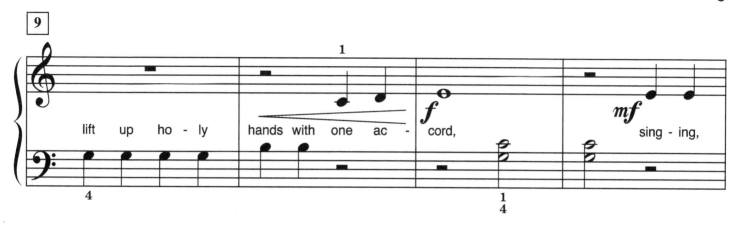

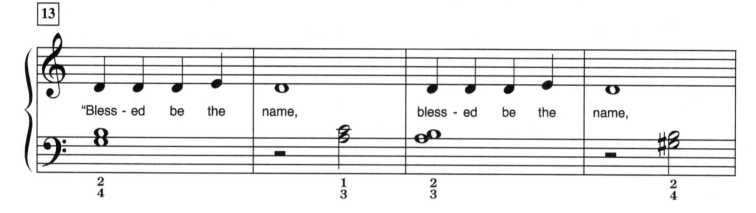

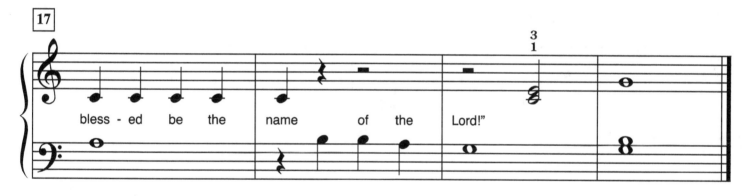

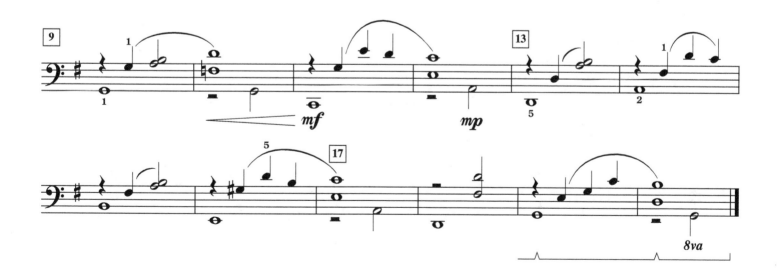

Use after page 19.

More Precious Than Silver

Words and Music by Lynn DeShazo

Arr. by Tom Gerou

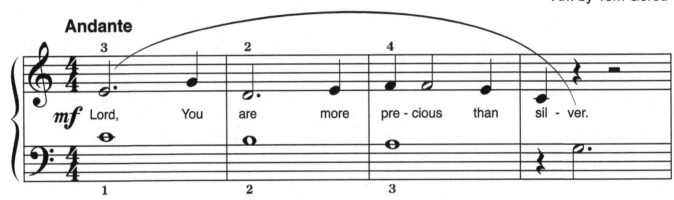

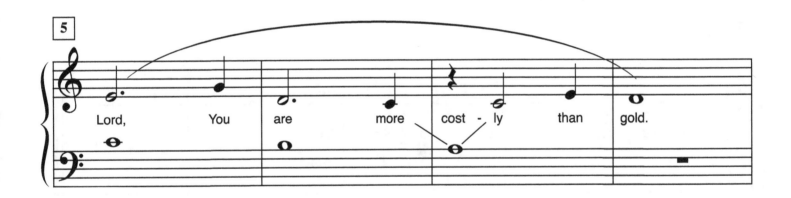

DUET PART (Student plays 1 octave higher.)

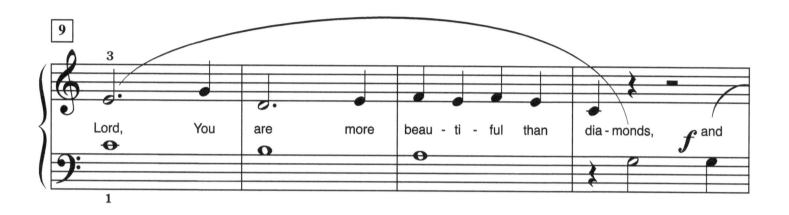

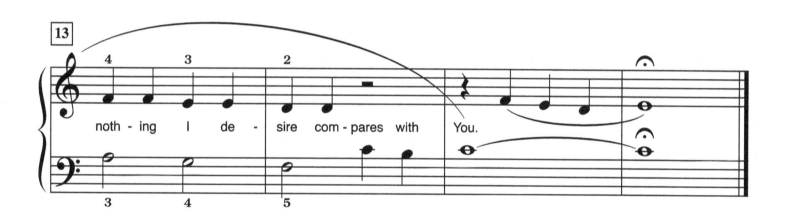

Use after page 21.

Amazing Grace
(My Chains Are Gone)

Words and Music by
Chris Tomlin and Louie Giglio
Arr. by Tom Gerou

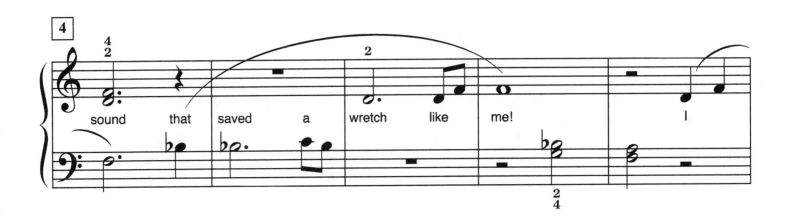

DUET PART (Student plays 1 octave higher.)

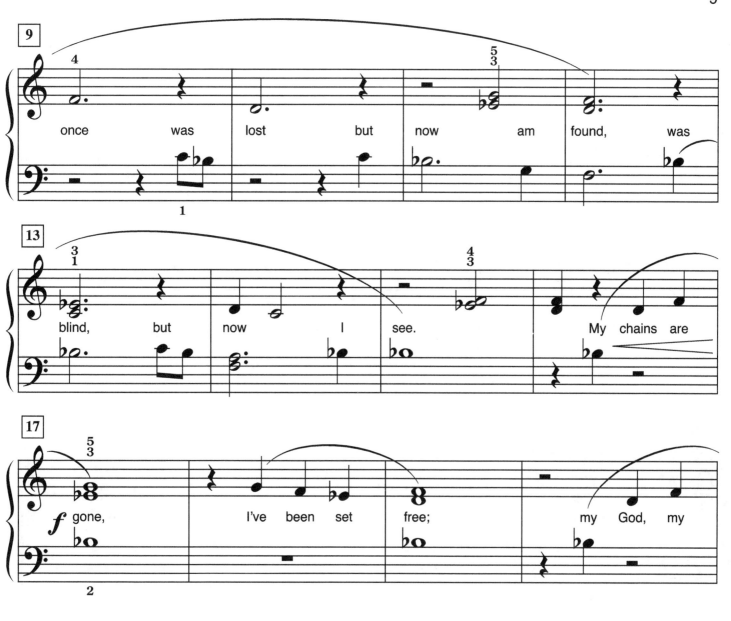

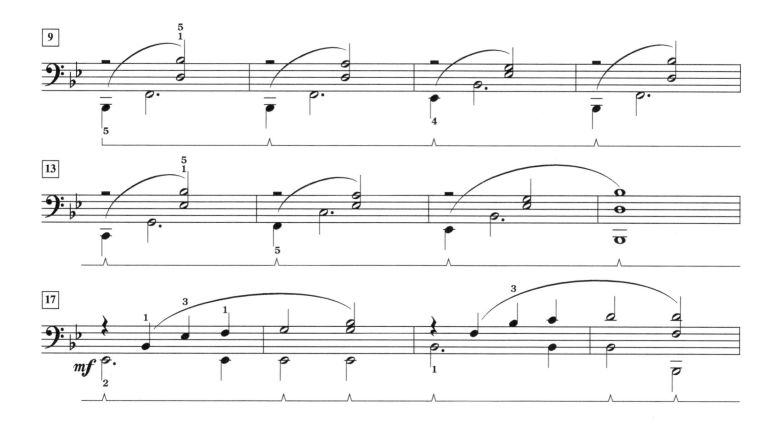

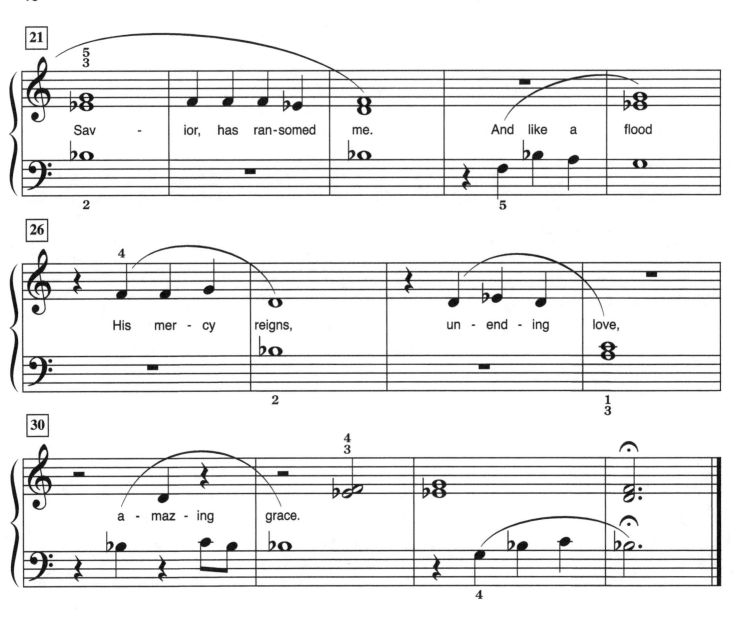

(DUET PART)

You Are My All in All

Words and Music by Dennis L. Jernigan
Arr. by Tom Gerou

DUET PART (Student plays 1 octave higher.)

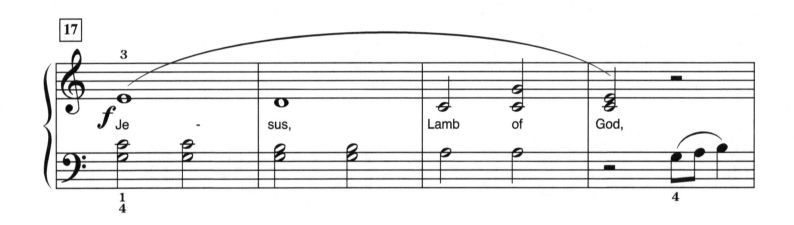

(DUET PART)

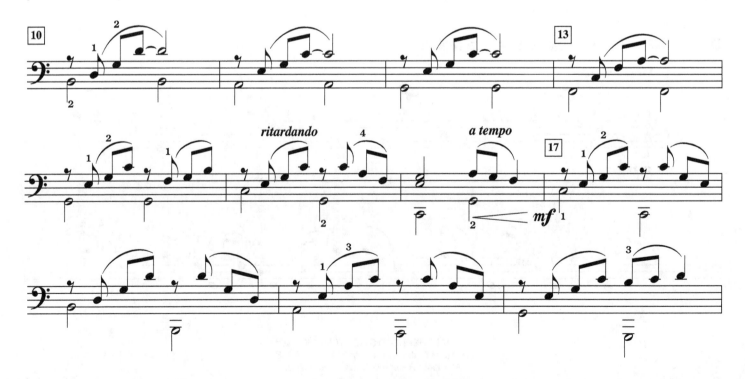

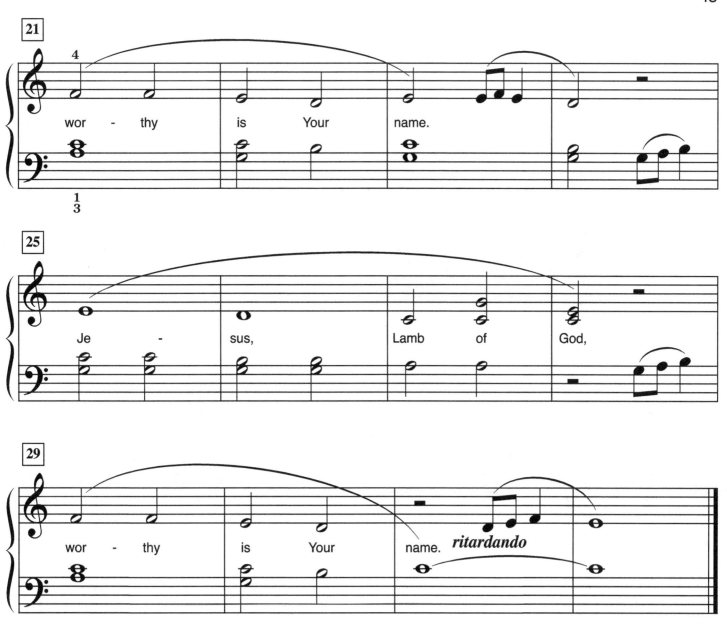

worthy is Your name.

Je - sus, Lamb of God,

worthy is Your name. *ritardando*

ritardando   *mp*

Use after page 28.

Shout to the Lord

Words and Music by Darlene Zschech
Arr. by Tom Gerou

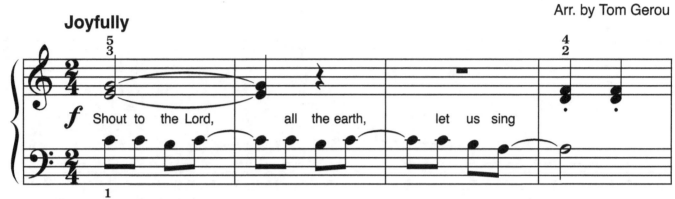

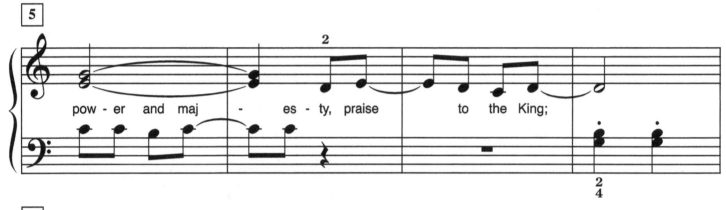

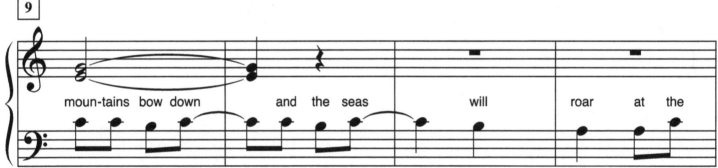

DUET PART (Student plays 1 octave higher.)

Use after pages 32–33.

How Great Is Our God

Words and Music by
Jesse Reeves, Chris Tomlin and Ed Cash

Arr. by Tom Gerou

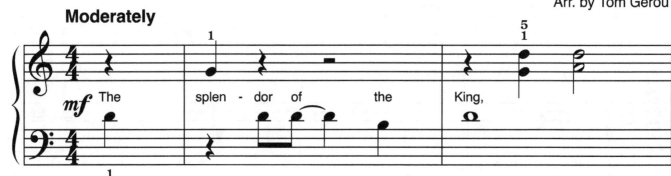

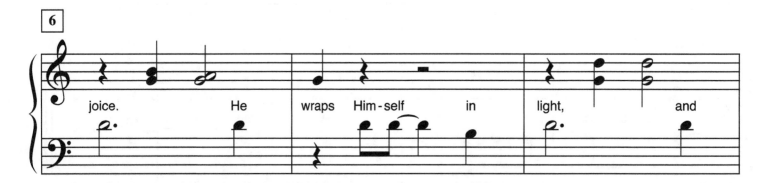

DUET PART (Student plays 1 octave higher.)

Use after pages 34–35.

As the Deer

Words and Music by Martin Nystrom
Arr. by Tom Gerou

DUET PART (Student plays 1 octave higher.)

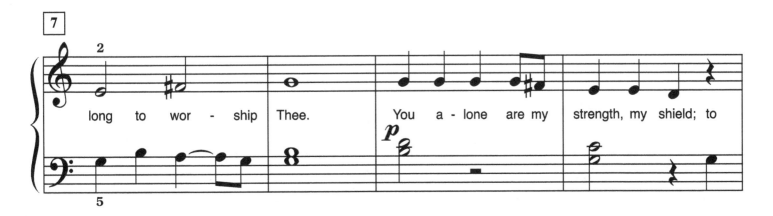

long to wor - ship Thee. You a - lone are my strength, my shield; to

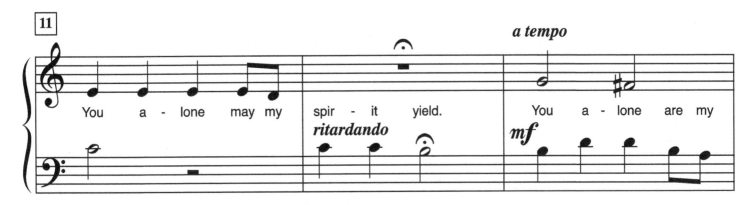

You a - lone may my spir - it yield. You a - lone are my

heart's de - sire and I long to wor - ship Thee.

Use after page 42.

Beautiful One

Words and Music by Tim Hughes
Arr. by Tom Gerou

Won - der-ful, so won - der-ful is Your un-fail - ing love. Your cross has spo - ken mer - cy o - ver me.

No eye has seen, no ear has heard, no heart could ful - ly

DUET PART (Student plays 1 octave higher.)

simile

Come, Now Is the Time to Worship

Words and Music by Brian Doerksen
Arr. by Tom Gerou

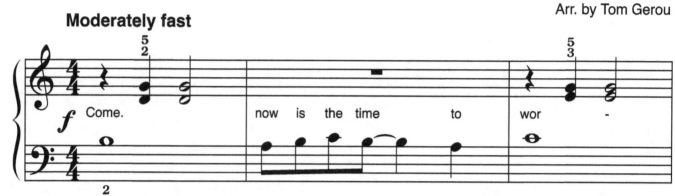

DUET PART (Student plays 1 octave higher.)

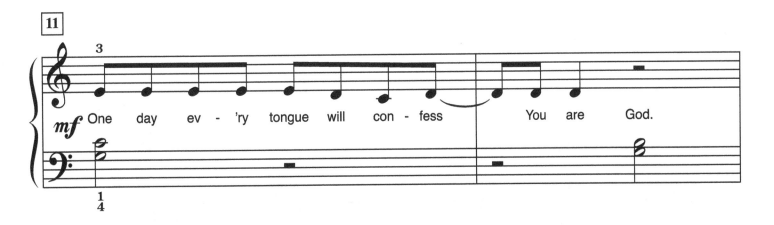

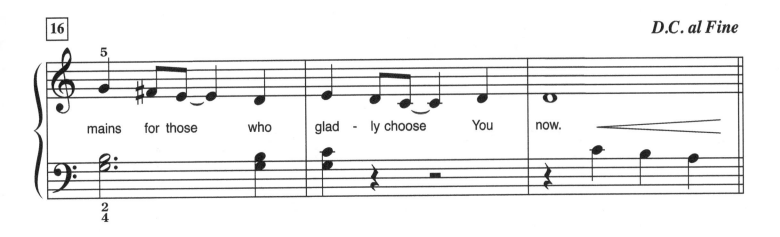

Use after pages 44–45.

Mighty Is Our God

Words and Music by
Don Moen, Eugene Greco and Gerrit Gustafson
Arr. by Tom Gerou

Moderately fast